Success Tweets

140 Bits of Common Sense
Career Success Advice
All in 140 Characters or Less

BUD BILANICH
The Common Sense Guy

Front Row Press
875 S. Colorado Blvd., #773 • Denver, CO 80246 • 303.393.0446

SUCCESS TWEETS

As always, this book is for Cathy
xoxoxoxoxoxoxoxoxoxoxoxoxoxoxoxoxoxoxoxo
xoxoxoxoxoxoxoxoxoxoxoxoxoxoxoxoxoxoxoxo
xoxoxoxoxoxoxoxoxoxoxoxoxoxoxoxoxoxoxoxo
xoxoxoxoxoxoxoxoxoxoxoxoxoxoxoxoxoxoxoxo
xoxoxoxoxoxoxoxoxoxoxoxoxoxoxoxoxoxoxoxo
xoxoxoxoxoxoxoxoxoxoxoxoxoxoxoxoxoxoxoxo
xoxoxoxoxoxoxoxoxoxoxoxoxoxoxoxoxoxoxoxo

That's 140 hugs and kisses…

Introduction

This is a success book, done as 140 tweets. It's a real book that will help you create the successful life and career you want and deserve.

It gives you 140 pieces of common sense career and life success advice, all in 140 characters or less.

It will tell you how to succeed in your life and career, one tweet at a time. You'll get the essentials with no fluff.

Creating the successful life and career you deserve should be fun and exciting. This book will show you how to do it.

Your time is valuable. You don't want to waste it. That's why you get 140 pieces of advice twitter style; in 140 characters or less.

If you want more in depth advice, go to http://www.CareerSuccessGPS.com and get the eBook version of my new book on career and life success.

Building a successful career is simple common sense. It's not hard, but you need to do it right.

Focus on the 4 Cs: Clarity, Commitment, Confidence, Competence.

Clarify the purpose and direction for your life and career.

- Create clarity by figuring out what success means to you personally.

- Create clarity by creating a vivid mental image of yourself as a success.

- Create clarity by determining your personal values.

Commit to taking personal responsibility for your life and career.

- Take personal responsibility by setting and achieving high goals.

- Take personal responsibility by choosing to react positively to the people and events in your life; especially the negative ones.

Build unshakeable self confidence.

- Build your confidence by choosing to be optimistic.

- Build your confidence by facing your fears and acting.

- Build your confidence by surrounding yourself with positive people.

- Build your confidence by finding a mentor to help you create your success.

- Build your confidence by sharing your knowledge and wisdom through mentoring others.

Get competent: create positive personal impact, become an outstanding performer, become a dynamic communicator, build strong relationships.

- Create positive personal impact by creating and nurturing your unique personal brand.

- Create positive personal impact by being impeccable in your presentation of self; in person and on line.

- Create positive personal impact by knowing and following the basic rules of business etiquette.

- Become an outstanding performer by keeping your skills up to date by becoming a lifelong learner.

- Become an outstanding performer by learning to manage your time and life.

- Become an outstanding performer by living a healthy lifestyle.

- Become a dynamic communicator by demonstrating strong conversation skills.

- Become a dynamic communicator by writing clearly and succinctly.

- Become a dynamic communicator by mastering public speaking skills.

- Build relationships through self awareness. Use this knowledge to better understand others.

- Build relationships by paying it forward; give with no expectation of return.

- Build relationships by using conflict to strengthen, not weaken, relationships with the people in your life.

The tweets that follow will show you how to put the 4 Cs to work — and create the successful life and career you want and deserve.

Will tweet books replace traditional books? Probably not. But this little book will get you started creating a successful life and career.

Enjoy this book. But remember, I want to talk *with* you, not *to* you. Please tweet what you think about my ideas. #BudBilanich

Each of the points I've made above is less than 140 characters.

See? You can communicate a lot of useful information in 140 characters or less. Enjoy the following 140 tweets.

Clarity

CLARITY

1

Define exactly what career and life success mean to you. It's easier to hit a clear, unambiguous target.

CLARITY

2

The more clear you are about what success means to you personally, the easier it will be to create the life and career you want.

CLARITY

3

Think of your purpose as your personal mission; why you are on this earth. Your direction is your vision for the next 3 to 5 years.

CLARITY

4

The mightier your purpose, the more likely you are to succeed. It will give you a strong foundation when the winds of change shift.

CLARITY

5

Your vision should be a BHAG; a Big Hairy Audacious Goal. Make it something that is really worth accomplishing.

CLARITY

6

Make sure that your personal mission and vision are what you want — not what someone else wants for you.

CLARITY

7

Figure out what you really want to do.
Work you love will make it easier to
create the successful life and career you
want and deserve.

CLARITY

8

Don't focus just on making money. If you do, you'll be asking too little of yourself. Focus on how you can be useful in this world.

CLARITY

9

Happiness doesn't come from getting more things. It comes from finding a worthy purpose and pursuing it.

CLARITY

10

Emerson says, "Good luck is another name for tenacity of purpose." Find your purpose and pursue it tenaciously.

CLARITY

11

Create a vivid mental image of yourself as a success. This vivid image will keep you motivated and moving forward when things get tough.

CLARITY

12

Visualization is powerful. The more vivid the image you have of your success, the more likely you are to succeed.

CLARITY

13

Your vivid mental image is a blueprint. It is a plan for success, but you still have to do the work to make it a reality.

CLARITY

14

Don't visualize the pain of failure. Visualize the euphoria of success.

CLARITY

15

Napoleon Hill on visualization: "What the mind can conceive and believe, it can achieve." What is your vision for your future?

CLARITY

16

Use affirmations to realize your vision of your success. Affirmations are statements about the future stated in the present tense.

CLARITY

17

Clarify your personal values. Your values
are your anchor. They ground you. They
center you. They keep you focused on
what's important.

CLARITY

18

You've got to stand for something, or you'll fall for anything. Your values help you make decisions in ambiguous situations.

CLARITY

19

Your personal values are things that you hold near and dear; things on which you absolutely will not compromise.

CLARITY

20

Your values come from deep inside you. Spend the time necessary to discover them. Then, hold fast to them. Honor them by your actions.

Commitment

COMMITMENT

21

You're in charge! Commit to taking personal responsibility for creating the successful life and career you want and deserve.

COMMITMENT

22

Set and achieve S.M.A.R.T. goals.
S.M.A.R.T. goals are Specific, Measurable,
Achievable, Relevant and Time Bound.

COMMITMENT

23

Goals are important. You can't get what you want if you don't know where you're going.

COMMITMENT

24

Focus on your goals several times a day. Spend your valuable time on the things that will help you achieve them.

COMMITMENT

25

List the reasons for each goal you set for yourself. These reasons will come in handy when you get tired and frustrated.

COMMITMENT

26

Keep your goals with you — in your wallet or on your screen saver. They will be a constant reminder of what you will achieve.

COMMITMENT

27

Create goals in all areas of your life: career, personal, business, family, hobbies, health and fitness. Make sure they are congruent.

COMMITMENT

28

Write your goals. Share them with others.
You are more likely to achieve goals that
you write and share.

COMMITMENT

29

Aim high. Set and achieve high goals —
month after month and year after year.
Do whatever it takes to achieve your
goals.

30

Success is a journey, not a destination. When you accomplish one goal, reach higher and set a new one.

COMMITMENT

31

Plan how you will achieve your goals. Then do whatever you have to do, not want or feel like doing, to achieve them.

COMMITMENT

32

Stuff happens as you go about creating a successful life and career. Choose to respond positively to the negative stuff that happens.

COMMITMENT

33

Take personal responsibility for your success. No one is going to do it for you. Adopt the motto, "If it's to be, it's up to me."

COMMITMENT

34

Treat failures as the tuition you pay to succeed. If you have a setback, choose to react positively and learn something.

COMMITMENT

35

Persistent people keep going; especially in the face of difficulties. Keep at it and you will accomplish your goals.

COMMITMENT

36

Don't be afraid to fail. You fail only if you don't learn something from the experience. Treat every failure as an opportunity to grow.

COMMITMENT

37

It's not what happens to you, but how you react to it. Don't dwell on the negative, use it as a springboard to action and creativity.

COMMITMENT

38

Don't let a slow day get you down. If you come back empty handed in your quest for success, get up the next day and keep working.

COMMITMENT

39

While other people and events have an
impact on your life, they don't shape it.
You get to choose how you react to
people and events.

COMMITMENT

40

Vision without action is a daydream. No matter how big your plans and dreams, they'll never become a reality until you act on them.

Confidence

CONFIDENCE

41

Focus on what you are becoming. This helps you believe in yourself and builds your confidence. Confidence is important to your success.

CONFIDENCE

42

Choose optimism. It builds your confidence. Believe that today will be better than yesterday and that tomorrow will be better yet.

CONFIDENCE

43

Optimism is contagious. Become a positive, optimistic person. Surround yourself with positive people. They will build your confidence.

CONFIDENCE

44

Be an optimist. Believe things will turn out well. When they don't, don't sulk. Learn what you can, use it the next time.

CONFIDENCE

45

Everyone is afraid sometime. Self confident people face their fears and act. Look your fears in the eye and do something.

CONFIDENCE

46

Four steps for dealing with fear that can sabotage your success: identify it, admit it, accept it, do something about it.

CONFIDENCE

47

Act. Feel the fear, and do it anyway. That's the definition of courage, and a great way to build your self confidence.

CONFIDENCE

48

Procrastination is the physical manifestation of fear and is a confidence killer. Act; especially when you're afraid.

CONFIDENCE

49

Surround yourself with positive people.
Hold them close. They will give you
energy and help you create the success
you want and deserve.

CONFIDENCE

50

Jettison the negative people in your life. They are energy black holes. They will suck you dry; but only if you let them.

CONFIDENCE

51

Find a mentor. Mentors are positive people who will help you find the lessons in your experiences and use them to move forward.

CONFIDENCE

52

Identify the self confident people you know. Pay attention to how they act and carry themselves. Watch what they do. Act like them.

CONFIDENCE

53

Act as if you expect to be accepted, and you will be. This will increase your confidence and help you make a strong personal impact.

CONFIDENCE

54

Fake it till you make it. Appear to be self confident and others will treat you as if you are. In turn, this will boost your confidence.

CONFIDENCE

55

Stand or sit up straight. Don't slouch.
Your mother was right. Good posture is
important. It makes you look self
confident.

CONFIDENCE

56

Self confidence must come from within.
Outside reinforcement and strokes can
help, but you have to build your own
confidence.

CONFIDENCE

57

Think only of the best, work only for the best and expect only the best. Forget the mistakes of the past. Press on to better things.

CONFIDENCE

58

Be as enthusiastic about the success of others as you are about your own. Help all people recognize that they are special.

CONFIDENCE

59

Give so much time to building your self confidence and improving yourself that you have no time to criticize others.

CONFIDENCE

60

Take stock of yourself. What are your strengths? What are your weaknesses? Confident people emphasize their strengths.

Competence

POSITIVE PERSONAL IMPACT

COMPETENCE

POSITIVE PERSONAL IMPACT

61

Create and nurture your unique personal brand. Stand, and be known for, something. Make sure that everything you do is on brand.

COMPETENCE

POSITIVE PERSONAL IMPACT

62

Your personal brand should be unique to you, but built on integrity. Integrity is doing the right thing when no one is looking.

COMPETENCE

POSITIVE PERSONAL IMPACT

63

Be visible. Volunteer for tough jobs. Brand yourself as a person who can and does make significant contributions.

COMPETENCE

POSITIVE PERSONAL IMPACT

64

Build your personal brand. Do whatever
it takes to make sure that people will
think of you in the way you want them to.

COMPETENCE

POSITIVE PERSONAL IMPACT

65

A good personal brand highlights your uniqueness. Be unconventional. Break rules.

COMPETENCE

POSITIVE PERSONAL IMPACT

66

Nurture your network. What your friends, colleagues and customers say about you is how others will think of your brand.

COMPETENCE

POSITIVE PERSONAL IMPACT

67

Demonstrate self respect. Be impeccable in your presentation of self — in person and on line.

COMPETENCE

POSITIVE PERSONAL IMPACT

68

Be well groomed and appropriate for every situation. Always dress one level up from what is expected. You'll stand out from the crowd.

COMPETENCE

POSITIVE PERSONAL IMPACT

69

Demonstrate respect for yourself and others in your dress. People will notice and respond positively to you.

COMPETENCE

POSITIVE PERSONAL IMPACT

70

"Business" is the first and most important word in "business casual." Dress like you're going to work, not a sporting event or club.

COMPETENCE

POSITIVE PERSONAL IMPACT

71

Observe successful people in your organization. What do they wear? Dress like them and you won't go wrong.

POSITIVE PERSONAL IMPACT

72

21st century technology has created new etiquette rules. Learn and use them to appear polished when you're on line.

COMPETENCE

POSITIVE PERSONAL IMPACT

73

Be gracious. Know and follow the basic rules of etiquette. Everybody likes to be around polite and mannerly people.

COMPETENCE

POSITIVE PERSONAL IMPACT

74

When someone compliments you, just say "thank you." When someone criticizes you, say "thank you, I'll work on that."

COMPETENCE

POSITIVE PERSONAL IMPACT

75

Learn and use simple table manners.
Good manners make you look polished
and poised.

COMPETENCE

POSITIVE PERSONAL IMPACT

76

Always act like a lady or gentleman. It's not old fashioned; it's smart business and leads to a successful life and career.

COMPETENCE

POSITIVE PERSONAL IMPACT

77

Keep your breath fresh. Brush after meals and coffee. Use the strips. Don't chew gum. Ever. It makes you look like a cow.

COMPETENCE

POSITIVE PERSONAL IMPACT

78

Say "thank you" often. You'll succeed, build a strong personal brand and leave a legacy of being a nice person.

COMPETENCE

POSITIVE PERSONAL IMPACT

79

Be courteous. It costs you nothing, and it can mean everything to someone else. It also helps in getting what you want.

COMPETENCE

POSITIVE PERSONAL IMPACT

80

Learn and use the basic rules of etiquette. Social faux pas might not ruin your career, but they certainly won't help it.

Competence

OUTSTANDING PERFORMANCE

COMPETENCE

OUTSTANDING PERFORMANCE

81

Become a lifelong learner. The half-life of knowledge is rapidly diminishing. Staying in the same place is the same as going backwards.

COMPETENCE

OUTSTANDING PERFORMANCE

82

Learn faster than the world changes. In a world that never stops changing, you can never stop learning and growing.

OUTSTANDING PERFORMANCE

83

Master your technical discipline. Share what you know. Become the go to person in your discipline in your company.

COMPETENCE

OUTSTANDING PERFORMANCE

84

Stay up to date on your industry. Read industry publications. Know the hot topics for your company, competitors and industry.

COMPETENCE

OUTSTANDING PERFORMANCE

85

Always be on the lookout for new ideas. Find opportunities where others see obstacles.

COMPETENCE

OUTSTANDING PERFORMANCE

86

Stay focused. Don't get distracted. Treat time as the precious commodity that it is. Manage your time and life well.

COMPETENCE

OUTSTANDING PERFORMANCE

87

Break large projects into smaller chunks. They are not so overwhelming that way. Set mini milestones for yourself.

COMPETENCE

OUTSTANDING PERFORMANCE

88

Get organized. Organize your time, life and workspace. Sweat the small stuff. Success is in execution. Execution is in the details.

COMPETENCE

OUTSTANDING PERFORMANCE

89

Create your own unique personal
organization system based on your needs
and what works for you.

COMPETENCE

OUTSTANDING PERFORMANCE

90

Positive time management is an important habit to develop. Habits are like muscles. The more you use them, the stronger they get.

COMPETENCE

OUTSTANDING PERFORMANCE

91

The better you feel, the better you'll
perform. Live a healthy lifestyle. Eat well.
Exercise regularly. Get regular checkups.

COMPETENCE

OUTSTANDING PERFORMANCE

92

Determine your peak energy times. Schedule high brain tasks when your energy is high and low brain tasks when it is low.

COMPETENCE

OUTSTANDING PERFORMANCE

93

Becoming a high performer is easier if you're physically fit. Increasing your heart rate is a great way to improve your fitness level.

COMPETENCE

OUTSTANDING PERFORMANCE

94

Don't take yourself too seriously. Lighten up. It will help you master yourself and become an outstanding performer.

COMPETENCE

OUTSTANDING PERFORMANCE

95

Get into a high performance mindset. Don't question yourself. Trust your skills and abilities.

COMPETENCE

OUTSTANDING PERFORMANCE

96

Good truly is the enemy of great. Don't settle for good performance. Today, good is mediocre. Become a great performer.

COMPETENCE

OUTSTANDING PERFORMANCE

97

Today, do the things others won't do; so tomorrow you can do the thing they can't do.

COMPETENCE

OUTSTANDING PERFORMANCE

98

Don't worry about getting credit for doing the job. Worry about getting the job done well — accurately and on time.

COMPETENCE

OUTSTANDING PERFORMANCE

99

Get the job done with what you've got. Don't worry about what you don't have or would like to have.

OUTSTANDING PERFORMANCE

100

Care about what you do. If you care a little, you'll be an OK performer. If you care a lot, you'll become an outstanding performer.

Competence
DYNAMIC COMMUNICATION

COMPETENCE

DYNAMIC COMMUNICATION

101

All dynamic communicators have mastered three basic communication skills: conversation, writing and presenting.

COMPETENCE

DYNAMIC COMMUNICATION

102

We're all in sales. You have to sell yourself every day. You need to become a dynamic communicator to sell your ideas.

DYNAMIC COMMUNICATION

103

Speak from your heart. Show that you care about yourself and the people with whom you are speaking.

COMPETENCE

DYNAMIC COMMUNICATION

104

Learn to handle yourself in conversation. A brief conversation with the right person can greatly help — or hinder — your career.

COMPETENCE

DYNAMIC COMMUNICATION

105

Conversation tips: be warm, pleasant, gracious and sensitive to the interpersonal needs and anxieties of others.

COMPETENCE

DYNAMIC COMMUNICATION

106

Demonstrate your understanding of others' points of view. Listen well and ask questions if you don't understand.

COMPETENCE

DYNAMIC COMMUNICATION

107

Become an excellent conversationalist by listening more than speaking. Pay attention to what other people say; respond appropriately.

COMPETENCE

DYNAMIC COMMUNICATION

108

Live people take precedence over phone
calls. Continue in person face to face
conversations, rather than answering
your cell phone.

DYNAMIC COMMUNICATION

109

Use the 2/3 – 1/3 rule. Listen two thirds
of the time; speak one third of the time.
Focus your complete attention on the
other person.

COMPETENCE

DYNAMIC COMMUNICATION

110

Remember and use people's names. Look for common ground with the people you meet. Find out about them, their hobbies and passions.

COMPETENCE

DYNAMIC COMMUNICATION

111

Become a clear, concise writer. Make your writing easy to read and understand. Use simple, straightforward language.

COMPETENCE

DYNAMIC COMMUNICATION

112

Explain jargon as you go along; or provide a glossary at the end of the document. Better yet, avoid jargon if at all possible.

COMPETENCE

DYNAMIC COMMUNICATION

113

Write clearly and simply: short words and sentences, first person, active voice. Be precise in your choice of words.

COMPETENCE

DYNAMIC COMMUNICATION

114

Use the active voice in your writing. Say "I suggest we do this," rather than "It is suggested that…"

COMPETENCE

DYNAMIC COMMUNICATION

115

Become an excellent presenter. Careers have been made on the strength of one or two good presentations.

COMPETENCE

DYNAMIC COMMUNICATION

116

Presentations are opportunities to shine. Don't let stage fright rob you of your opportunity. Get control of your nerves.

COMPETENCE

DYNAMIC COMMUNICATION

117

Presentation steps: 1) Determine the message. 2) Analyze the audience. 3) Organize the information. 4) Design visuals. 5) Practice.

118

Presentations are easy to create. Write your closing first, your opening next. Then fill in the content. Practice, practice, practice.

COMPETENCE

DYNAMIC COMMUNICATION

119

Discipline yourself to prepare for presentations. Practice out loud until you are totally in sync with what you're going to say.

COMPETENCE

DYNAMIC COMMUNICATION

120

Practice presentations. You can control your nerves by practicing out loud. The more you practice, the less afraid you'll be.

Competence
RELATIONSHIP BUILDING

COMPETENCE

RELATIONSHIP BUILDING

121

Get genuinely interested in others. Help bring out the best in everyone you know. Others will gravitate to you.

COMPETENCE

RELATIONSHIP BUILDING

122

Keep confidences and avoid gossip. Don't embarrass others by repeating what they share with you — even if it isn't in confidence.

COMPETENCE

RELATIONSHIP BUILDING

123

Use every social interaction to build and strengthen relationships. Strong relationships are your ticket to success.

COMPETENCE

RELATIONSHIP BUILDING

124

Everyone has something to offer. Never dismiss anyone out of hand. Take the initiative. Actively build relationships.

RELATIONSHIP BUILDING

125

Get to know yourself. Use your self knowledge to better understand others and build mutually beneficial relationships with them.

COMPETENCE

RELATIONSHIP BUILDING

126

Self awareness is the first step in building relationships and resolving conflict.

COMPETENCE

RELATIONSHIP BUILDING

127

Pay it forward. Build relationships by giving with no expectation of return. Give of yourself to build strong relationships.

COMPETENCE

RELATIONSHIP BUILDING

128

When meeting someone new ask yourself, "What can I do to help this person?" You'll build stronger relationships by thinking this way.

COMPETENCE

RELATIONSHIP BUILDING

129

There is no quid pro quo in effective relationships. Do for others without being asked or waiting for them to do for you.

COMPETENCE
RELATIONSHIP BUILDING

130

Be generous. By giving with no expectation of return, you'll be surprised by how much comes back to you in the long run.

COMPETENCE

RELATIONSHIP BUILDING

131

Be happy to see others succeed. Use the success of others to motivate you to greater success.

COMPETENCE

RELATIONSHIP BUILDING

132

Trust is the glue that holds relationships together. The more you demonstrate trust in others the more they will trust you.

COMPETENCE

RELATIONSHIP BUILDING

133

Resolve conflict positively. Treat conflict as an opportunity to strengthen, not destroy, the relationships you've worked hard to build.

COMPETENCE

RELATIONSHIP BUILDING

134

Settle disputes and resolve differences quickly. Don't let them drag on. Engage the other person in meaningful conversation.

COMPETENCE

RELATIONSHIP BUILDING

135

Be a consensus builder. Focus on where you agree with others. It will be easier to resolve differences and create agreement.

COMPETENCE

RELATIONSHIP BUILDING

136

Be responsible for yourself. No one can "make you angry." Choose to act in a civil, constructive manner in tense situations.

COMPETENCE

RELATIONSHIP BUILDING

137

Do your job; give credit to others for doing theirs. Everyone likes to work with people who share the credit for a job well done.

COMPETENCE

RELATIONSHIP BUILDING

138

We all make mistakes. Own up to yours. You'll become known as a straight shooter, honest with yourself and others.

COMPETENCE

RELATIONSHIP BUILDING

139

Become widely trusted. Deliver on what you say you'll do. If you can't meet a commitment, let the other person know right away.

COMPETENCE

RELATIONSHIP BUILDING

140

Social networks allow you to help others.
Give value; and you'll be able to build
some great online relationships.

141

Knowing is not enough. Successful people will read the advice in these tweets. And they will act on it. Be a successful person.

Now that you've read these 140 tweets on life and career success, you may want to read more on the subject. That's why I've decided to give you a gift — several in fact.

If you go to http://www.SuccessTweets.com/freegifts and register you will receive links to download the eBook versions of three of my most popular books on the topic of life and career success:

- *Straight Talk for Success*
- *Star Power: Common Sense Ideas for Career and Life Success*
- *I Want YOU...To Succeed*

I will include the audio book version of *Straight Talk for Success,* and a set of digital mem-cards that highlight the information in *Straight Talk.*

Also, I will send you 25 of my best success tips in audio form. You'll get two a week for 12½ weeks.

Finally, you will begin receiving my weekly ezine, and daily success quotes.

I really want you to create the life and career success you want and deserve. That's why I wrote *Success Tweets,* and that's why I'm giving you these other gifts.

Just go to http://www.SuccessTweets.com/freegifts, enter your name and email address, and you'll be directed to a page where you can download all of the free gifts.

Bud Bilanich
May 2010
Denver Colorado USA
www.BudBilanich.com

Success Tweets makes a great gift!

Quantity discounts are available
from the publisher.

Call 303.393.0446 to inquire
about quantity pricing.

Made in the USA
Charleston, SC
23 September 2010